MAKE YOUR OWN PICTURE STORIES FOR KIDS
WITH ASD (AUTISM SPECTRUM DISORDER)

of related interest

The Kids' Guide to Staying Awesome and In Control
Simple Stuff to Help Children Regulate
their Emotions and Senses
Lauren Brukner
Illustrated by Apsley
ISBN 978 1 84905 997 8
eISBN 978 0 85700 962 3

The Panicosaurus
Managing Anxiety in Children Including
Those with Asperger Syndrome
K.I. Al-Ghani
Illustrated by Haitham Al-Ghani
ISBN 978 8 4905 356 3
eISBN 978 0 85700 706 3

The Disappointment Dragon
Learning to cope with disappointment (for all children and
dragon tamers, including those with Asperger Syndrome)
K.I. Al-Ghani
Illustrated by Haitham Al-Ghani
ISBN 978 1 84905 432 4
eISBN 978 0 85700 780 3

The Red Beast
Controlling Anger in Children with Asperger's Syndrome
K.I. Al-Ghani
Illustrated by Haitham Al-Ghani
ISBN 978 1 84310 943 3
eISBN 978 1 84642 848 7

MAKE YOUR OWN PICTURE STORIES FOR KIDS WITH ASD (AUTISM SPECTRUM DISORDER)

A DIY Guide for Parents and Carers

Brian Attwood

Jessica Kingsley *Publishers*
London and Philadelphia

First published in 2015
by Jessica Kingsley Publishers
73 Collier Street
London N1 9BE, UK
and
400 Market Street, Suite 400
Philadelphia, PA 19106, USA

www.jkp.com

Library of Congress Cataloging in Publication Data
Attwood, Brian (Brian Christopher)
Make your own picture stories for kids with ASD (autism spectrum disorder) : a
DIY guide for parents
and carers / Brian Attwood.
pages cm
ISBN 978-1-84905-638-0 (alk. paper)
1. Autistic children--Behavior modification. 2. Picture books for children--
Authorship. 3. Narrative
therapy. 4. Parents of autistic children. I. Title.
RJ506.A9A8687 2015
618.92'89165--dc23
2014042546

British Library Cataloguing in Publication Data
A CIP catalogue record for this book is available from the British Library

ISBN 978 1 84905 638 0
eISBN 978 1 78450 117 4

Printed and bound in the United States

CONTENTS

ACKNOWLEDGEMENTS

Behind even the smallest and simplest book there is often a large number of people who, knowingly or otherwise, have contributed to its creation.

So it is in this case and with apologies for any thoughtless omissions, these are my unsung heroines and heroes:

Angela Birch, Lynda Wallis, Kate Turnbull, Carol Kerrigan, Caroline Wright and Cathy Rose for enriching John's life (and ours) with daytime respite care, professional good sense and providing him with a wider social life.

To the McKenna clan, Cameron Ross and Grace Brazer for many hours of 'sitting' and the volunteers at SNAP Hemel Hempstead.

To all at The Collett School in Hemel for the special needs education they provide our son. Also: staff at John's previous school, St Thomas More in Berkhamsted, for their remarkable and exemplary efforts to accommodate John's needs in a mainstream environment; Kaye Wilson from Marlin Montessori;

and Father John Boland, John Wright and others at Sacred Heart Roman Catholic Church.

Production-wise, thanks to my former colleague at The Stage newspaper, Sarah Rogers, for designing my original manuscript, to my commissioning editor Rachel Menzies, production editor Kate Mason and all at Jessica Kingsley Publishers.

Lastly, our family: To my mother Nell Attwood for her knowledge and for urging me to write the book and to my daughter Eve for dedication and love way beyond the normal duties of a Big Sister. Pride of place, however, goes to my wife Lisa, who remains deservedly the most constant and loved presence in John's life, who had the foresight to hold on to every one of my cartoon stories and who pushed me to write this volume.

And, of course, I should add the person without whom none of this would have happened – our son John who has both challenged us and enriched our lives. I hope we shall continue to return the favour.

Introduction

Our son John was in his nursery year at school when he was diagnosed as being on the autistic spectrum.

Since then, thanks to the efforts of dedicated staff in the mainstream school he attended and the special needs school he now attends – plus his mother, sister, grandmother and countless relatives and friends – John's development has been considerable.

But problems persist: John's use of verbal language remains very selective, his attention span is short and his ability to cope with the unpredictability of life is limited. Changes to routines and the unexpected unsettle him, as they do many ASD kids.

Stories using pictures and other images with a limited amount of words have made a huge difference in helping John and other children to deal with these situations. Fortunately, a wide range of books, flashcards and online resources is now available to help parents and carers.

The problem is, there will never be enough of them to deal with every challenge that arises; there's a limit to how many books parents can buy, and every situation will be different.

Let's remember, too, that every child is different. There will be never be a book available for every occasion, let alone one that can speak to your child's individual needs in every circumstance. When it comes to your child, no volume is likely to match the in-depth knowledge that you possess as a parent or carer.

If only you could harness that knowledge in a completely individual story made for your child.

You can.

CHAPTER 1

The Answer Lies in Your Hands

Some years back, my wife and I (and John's older sister, Eve) were in the grip of another John meltdown.

Keen to help my wife who was bearing the brunt of it, I took a pen and a sheet of A4 paper and began doing my own story. Simple little figures, the shortest sentences, with as many of those words as possible in speech bubbles or images. A straightforward narrative that explained what was happening, what the end result would be, and depicting a happy, safe outcome.

It took time to get his attention but we started to read it slowly to him, John joined in and began smiling. He calmed down. He understood.

We didn't realise straight away what we had stumbled on. It took several more such tantrums before we started to make our picture stories a first, rather than a last, resort.

After a while they became second nature. So when we knew we had a visit to relations pending, a trip to the London Transport Museum (a John favourite), or a start at a 'new school', the picture stories were read to John the night before.

When there was a sudden change (cancelling a train ride because of line problems, missing out on the school zoo trip due to illness) the story was drawn in order to break the news – with John rather than us reading it out.

In our experience it doesn't work 100% of the time – just in a majority of cases in which we employ hand-written stories. And if it works for us, the chances are that it can work for you and your loved ones/charges.

You just have to be able to DRAW.

CHAPTER 2

It's Easier Than You Think

"But I can't draw."

That's the usual reaction. But think about that statement…

What you almost certainly mean is not that you *can't* draw but that you can't draw very *well*.

Sure, you can't draw like Turner or Rembrandt. Perhaps you can't even draw like a talented ten-year-old. Maybe you can't depict a realistic-looking face or body.

OK, but…

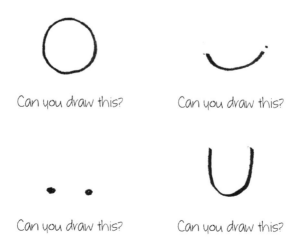

Can you draw this?   Can you draw this?

Can you draw this?   Can you draw this?

Can you draw this?

Can you draw this?

Can you draw this?

Can you draw this?

Let's try again…

You've just run out of excuses.

Doubtless someone will point out, "That's so simple, a child of six could have done it!"

Agreed, it's not hard and yes, nearly anyone can do it. So what? It isn't great art but that's *not* the point of it. It's about **communication** – a simple, visual tool that's easy to draw and easy to understand. The central fact is that, in our experience, it *works*.

"But that doesn't look like me, I'm…

etc. etc. etc."

Sorry, but it doesn't matter. Once again: this is about communicating a message, creating happy outcomes. It's not about capturing your best side or anyone else's or demonstrating your latent artistic talent.

Here's John and I together…

I'm the 6-foot-plus guy with the grey hair. John's the handsome ten-year-old on the right. I've yet to hear John complain about the similarity in our graphic representation and doubt that I ever shall. Of course it *may* be that your loved one likes a tad more realism, but until you know it, wait for demand and keep it simple. It's easier and it's quicker this way, and that's what you want and need.

CHAPTER 3

Stick Your Toe in the Water

So, drawing is merely a means to achieve your end – which is to reduce fear and uncertainty in your child. The message is what's important.

Yet you need to practice using the tools. For this, all you need is:

- Some sheets of plain paper (A4 minimum but for practice, A3 is best)

- A pencil ('B' grade with a decent point).

Most of us tend to grip tight when writing but, when drawing, hold the pencil as lightly as you can. Don't force it on the page. *Coax* it round, like so:

if you're drawing a circle.

When you draw a line it doesn't need to be unbroken or heavy.

EXERCISE

- Draw all the individual parts of your human figures. One entire page.
- Next put them together to construct an actual figure. One entire page.

Keep your pencil motion light and easy. No heavy pressure, let it flow.

This is a practice session, so don't waste time erasing any supposed mistakes. Cover your page in circles, lines and dots until you can do these without thinking. Just imagine you're doodling on a notebook – it's no different.

Now let's think about some other components.

Human emotions

We shall want to convey some basic emotions such as happy, sad, excited or upset. Here are some ways to do these:

Mouth up (happy), mouth down (sad).

Excited – two foot bounces with a line for the ground. With the appropriate up/down mouth this can convey joy or anger.

Tearful – comma style teardrops.

Shouting/tantrum – radiating lines, open mouth.

Movement

Running – front foot pointing diagonally upwards, back foot straight down. Motion lines after moving person/object.

Hailing/greeting – arms raised.

Places

Home, school, cinema, church, shop, you name it –
most need little more than a square or rectangle and a
descriptive word.

Destinations

You've seen them in comics. A single word written on
a thick arrow says we are travelling towards 'school'.
Embellish it if you like with a vertical post and
ground line.

Other living things and toy animals

John's favourite toy, without which he never travels, is a soft rabbit named Bunny. When I draw Bunny, then, like John does, I look at him as another person – just one with longer ears:

Objects

Vehicles are a must of course, but they needn't be much more than rectangles with circles in the case of a car:

…or indeed a train.

EXERCISE

Draw:

- A page full of the following emotions: happy, sad, angry, upset
- A page full of running, jumping figures conveying those emotions
- A page full of the places, objects and destinations that mean most to your child (you're the best judge).

CHAPTER 4

Words Are Pictures Too

The constant theme is that your drawings are there to communicate a message rather than wow admirers. They function like a special form of words.

But when you use words, you need to think how they, too, can be more like pictures. Use as few as possible, but use them effectively.

If you want a word to stand out, it's not difficult. You can:

- Capitalise it ZOO

- Bold it **ZOO**

- Underline it <u>ZOO</u>

- Colour it ZOO

- Make it come alive ZOO

Exclamations are often overused, but in picture stories they are an asset:

Today we are going to the...

ZOO!

Tip: Just be careful when you use this. With **ZOO!** it will probably be fail-safe. The same does not apply to **DENTIST!** In which instance you need to focus on positive outcomes (see Chapter 5).

Speech bubbles

Speech bubbles deserve a section of their own. They lift the words off the page and give life to emotions. They also give the reader a greater sense of being part of the story.

Thus, if I want to convey John will be pleased with an outcome, I don't simply state it; I show him saying it.

They aren't hard to draw. Just do a circle but don't quite finish it.

Make sure the opening is closest to the person speaking.

Draw a dot quite close to the person.

Draw a line (straight or curved) from one end of the unfinished circle to that dot.

Then draw another line from the dot to the other end of the unfinished circle.

There's your speech bubble.

    However: *before* you draw your speech bubble, write the words you want to put inside it.

If you don't, you might run out of space to fit the words in.

EXERCISE

- Try some word highlighting: zoo, circus, cinema, station
- Draw speech bubbles for the following: Hooray! That was fun! It's good to be safe!
- Make up your own but aim for as few words as possible

CHAPTER 5

✳ ✳ ✳

From Single Image to Story

You've mastered the basics of drawing simple images, but now you need to put those skills together to create a story.

This is where your unique knowledge as the parent/carer of your particular child kicks in: when it comes to the situations they find most challenging, you are the expert.

And while every situation and every child is different, like film scripts, they can be reduced at the start to certain common situations. Learn to address some of these, and you can quickly branch out to all kinds of variations.

In my experience the most frequent tend to be:

- Issues of appropriate/inappropriate behaviour

- Routines

- Changes to regular routines

- Reassurance needed

- Key events

- Abstract matters (e.g. loss of a loved one).

These are very different situations but the basic approach you take needs to be the same and can be summed up with the initials **IDC**:

> **Identify** the situation
>
> **Describe** how will it unfold/ how will we behave/ deal with it?
>
> **Convey** a positive outcome.

The last element mustn't be overlooked. You need to let your child know not only what will happen, but give them a sense that the outcome will be good – or at least safe and unthreatening. A speech bubble conveying a happy sentiment is one method. It might help to see some of ours (see Chapter 6).

It's also important to tie up loose ends. If a child has to leave a special object or toy at home, reinforce the idea that it will be waiting for them when they return. You'll see examples in the next chapter.

CHAPTER 6

Here's Some I Made Earlier

Some of the stories you will see here were planned well beforehand; others were sketched out minutes before John saw them; others have been sketched in the midst of a meltdown. Here's a brief description of what you will find.

School

'Leaving school' – John switched from his mainstream school to a special school half way through the week. He needed a countdown and a happy conclusion.

'Starting school' – when he began his introduction to his new school, John needed to know who he would see and that everything would be all right.

'Going to new school' – the school day needs a routine and order, plus reassurance that any item or person left at home will be there for him when he returns.

'No sandals' – John didn't want to stop wearing sandals when term time began. School rules say he must wear shoes. So I present this as a direct request to John from his head teacher.

'Special trip' – school trip means a change in routine, different clothes and different bags. The new routine needs spelling out, together with the idea that it is special and fun and will end happily back at home.

Home

'Only 6 DVDs' – John prefers not to travel light. Persuading him not to take bag-loads of toys and DVDs can be difficult. He needs preparing for a limit on the amount of items he has.

'Can't play' – John's long-suffering big sister needed a break from entertaining him on the Wii. We needed to persuade him to take a lead in 'telling' Eve not to play.

'Cancelled event' – bad weather meant a last-minute cancellation of John's SNAP playgroup. John had to be aware of why he couldn't go and be content with the outcome.

'The day Grandpa died' – Grandpa was a regular part of John's life so we needed to explain what his death meant in a down-to-earth way he could understand.

<u>Finishing mainstream school, starting special school - 1</u>

This week John goes to a NEW SCHOOL! 😊

On Monday -
John still goes to the Thomas More School

 Thomas More   3 more days!

On Tuesday -
John still goes to the Thomas More School

Thomas More   2 more days!

On Wednesday -
John still goes to the Thomas More School

 Thomas More   Last day!

Today is his last day. Time to say GOODBYE!

CLASSMATES

TEACHERS

<u>Finishing mainstream school,
starting special school - 2</u>

On Thursday - First day at new school - The Collett School!

LATER... MUM PICKS JOHN UP EARLY

Finishing mainstream school, starting special school - 3

When we wake up...

... John is going to his new school

School

John will go to school in the big taxi with the children

So...
we need to be ready QUICKLY!

① We   eat breakfast

② We   put on our uniform

③   We do wee and teeth

When the taxi comes...   The taxi!

John takes...
school bag
coat
water bottle

...Bunny goes in his bag but everything else stays at home

See you later!

When school is finished, John goes home in the taxi. Mum and Eve and all his things are waiting!

John's things

Hi John!

Hooray! I had fun!

No sandals in school

Tomorrow... we go back to school and see our friends

Mr Hoult-Allen, the head teacher, has a special message for John

Hi John!

Dear John,
When we go to school
I want you to wear your
special school shoes
       from,
          Mr Hoult-Allen

To John

What does it say?

Play = sandals
School = shoes

So, in the morning we eat breakfast
watch iPad
and get dressed

school clothes

At 7.20 we turn iPad...

OFF!

We do wee and teeth

Toothpaste

Then we go in the taxi to school

TAXI!!

shoes

After school we come...
Home to Mum!
Hooray!

Hi John!

School trip

Today, it is John's VERY SPECIAL TRIP!

But where are we going?

TO LEGOLAND!

In the morning we don't wear school uniform
we wear our P.E. shirt and our own trousers

AND we put on our SUNCREAM

Bunny stays at home with school bag and lunch bag
and they wait with Mummy

John goes in the school
taxi with Sarah and his
new rucksack

We don't mind, have a nice time, John!

Hi John, I am looking after your lunch and your swimming things for splashing!

When we get to school, we take special taxis to

LEGOLAND! HOORAY!

John will stay with his friends and the
grown-ups... he won't get lost.

He will have a very happy day.

HAPPY!

Then we go back to school. Mum and Dad will take John home.

Dad Mum Eve Bunny

Hi John!

Hi! I had such
a great time
everyone!

Only 6 DVDs

Today, John is going to Angie's house

When we go to Angie's house we take...

And we only take 6 DVDs in 1 bag

We don't take lots of bags

and we don't take more than 6 DVDS

She can't play with you

Poor Eve has hurt her hand

She has played too much Wii

Now she has a big bandage

The doctor says

We have to do what the
doctor tells us, says John

John tells Eve:

Eve says:

John tells Mum and Dad:

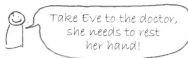

Good idea, John

Playgroup cancelled

It is Saturday and the roads are icy

The car park at SNAP has <u>too much</u> ice

Everyone slipped...   Lizzie fell over

Tell the mums and dads not to come today

So we will all stay home and go next time –
it's too icy and we don't want to
fall and get hurt, says John

The day Grandpa died

Grandpa Ray has
not been very well
for a long, long time.

Today Grandpa died,
which was sad.
Everybody cried.

But if you look at Grandpa,
you can see he is sleeping
nicely and is happy.

We can be happy too
because Grandpa isn't
ill anymore.

And we have a lot to remember him with.

You'll see plenty that you would have done differently and/or could have improved on. If so, then so much the better, because now it's your turn.

CHAPTER 7

Over to You

Here are some situations that may be familiar to you. Try to complete each one without interruption. After all, when a crisis does break, writer's or artist's block will be a luxury you can't afford. The more you stick with it, the faster you will master the process.

So far, you may have been working on A3 paper. I recommend you try to use A4 now – it forces you to keep your stories short, and the chances are that when problems arise and you need a scrap to write on in a hurry, it's more likely to be that size.

SO HERE ARE YOUR CHALLENGES

1. A cancelled fun outing
2. Can't wear favourite jacket
3. Being quiet/good in the library/at wedding service/ supermarket
4. Buying new shoes
5. Taking turns

CHAPTER 8

Against the Clock

By now you should be certain of two things:

1. You can draw – at least well enough for the task in hand.

2. You can put words and images into a picture story for most situations.

However, there's one missing ingredient. The need for picture stories arises in three different scenarios. Those you can prepare for well in advance, those you need to tackle with minutes to spare, and those that need addressing right away. The first of these you can deal with pretty well now, but what about the second and third? There's only one way to find out…

TIME CHALLENGE!

You've done the exercises. Now do these two in ten minutes:

- Cancelled trip
- Non-uniform day at school.

Now do them again immediately, without looking at your previous efforts.

CHAPTER 9

Not the End but Perhaps the End of the Beginning

As I've proven, this process is not rocket science and it doesn't take a great deal of talent. Plus, most of the skill relies on you harnessing your own considerable knowledge.

The other thing, as none of you need to be told, is that this is no miracle solution to the ongoing problems you and your child face every day of your lives.

The best I can promise is that it will make a little bit of your lives a tad easier, *sometimes*. It can prove unsuccessful on occasions, but we do remain surprised just how often it does make some situations easier that used to be so very hard.

I hope you'll find the same applies to you and yours.

Brian Attwood

The Conversation Train
A Visual Approach to
Conversation for Children
on the Autism Spectrum
Joel Shaul

Hardback: £14.99 / $24.95
ISBN: 978 1 84905 986 2 (US/Canada)
ISBN: 978 1 84905 531 4 (UK/World)
72 pages

This inventive color picture book uses the metaphor of a train to teach basic conventions of conversation to children with autism spectrum disorders (ASDs).

Locomotives are like greetings; they get the train going. Train cars are like different speakers' turns; it is good to have at least a few when you are in conversation. A switch track is like a tactful change in the topic of conversation. When a conversation veers off-topic it is like a derailed train. As well as attractive color photographs of trains, the book contains engaging photocopiable worksheets and coloring pages to help promote skill generalization.

This highly visual approach to conversation is ideally suited to children with ASDs aged approximately 5-13.

Joel Shaul is a Licensed Clinical Social Worker who specializes in ASDs. Through his organization, Autism Teaching Strategies, he provides workshops on social skills teaching and mental health treatment methods. He is also co-creator of Ryuu social skills products. He provides clinical and consultation services at The Watson Institute of Sewickley, PA. Joel's website can be found at www.autismteachingstrategies.com.

The Green Zone Conversation Book
Finding Common Ground in
Conversation for Children on
the Autism Spectrum
Joel Shaul

Hardback: £18.99 / $29.95
ISBN: 978 1 84905 759 2
96 pages

In conversation, children on the autism spectrum often struggle to select topics of interest to others. Many have strong, narrow interests and feel compelled to introduce these subjects when they talk.

This book provides a simple visual model to help children experience more success in finding common ground in conversation. The "Green Zone" is a visual representation of finding common ground between one person (blue) and another person (yellow) to create a "green zone" that represents the pair's shared interests. The book, illustrated with hundreds of photographs representing the range of other people's interests, clearly explains what the "Green Zone" is and how to find it, and contains many photocopiable conversation practice activities and reinforcement worksheets based on this simple visual.

Ideal for use in classroom settings or at home, this attractive, full colour book is suitable for children on the autism spectrum aged 7 and up.

Joel Shaul is a Licensed Clinical Social Worker who specializes in ASDs. Through his organization, Autism Teaching Strategies, he provides workshops on social skills teaching and mental health treatment methods. He is also co-creator of Ryuu social skills products. He provides clinical and consultation services at The Watson Institute of Sewickley, PA. Joel's website can be found at www.autismteachingstrategies.com.

Talk to Me
Conversation Strategies for Parents
of Children on the Autism Spectrum
or with Speech and Language Impairments
Heather Jones

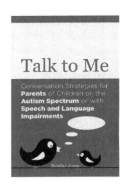

Paperback: £12.99 / $19.95
ISBN: 9781849054287
168 pages

If your child finds talking to people a struggle, this is the book to get the conversation started.

In this hands-on guide, Heather Jones offers practical advice, born of experience with her own son, which will help you teach your child the principles of communication. Full of strategies and examples, it shows how you can allay fears, build confidence and teach your child to enjoy conversation. Once a child gets used to talking with other people, many life skills can develop more easily as they grow up – from making friends and shopping for themselves, to being interviewed and eventually getting a job.

This handy book provides guidance and inspiration to parents, teachers and anyone else who cares for a child who finds language and comprehension difficult.

Heather Jones's son, Jamie, has Asperger Syndrome and severe speech and language impairments. When Jamie was 10, Heather stumbled across a way of getting through to him. Over the years she developed this methodology in more detail, calling it conversational therapy, and has never looked back. Jamie is now 19 and can hold a conversation, which has enabled him to go on to achieve much more, including passing his driving test and getting a job. Heather is the Director of Milkwood Educational, which publishes ESL textbooks in the Far East. She lives in Queensland, Australia.